WHAT'S COOKING
IN
MARGIE'S KITCHEN

Margie Gaunt

BookLocker

Trenton, Georgia

Copyright © 2021 Margie Gaunt

Print ISBN: 978-1-64719-823-7
Ebook ISBN: 978-1-64719-824-4

Published by BookLocker.com, Inc., Trenton, Georgia, U.S.A.

Printed on acid-free paper.

BookLocker.com, Inc.
2021

This is my first cookbook of many of my favorite recipes. There is a mixture of all sorts of yummy things from seasonings, appetizers, salad, side, casseroles and desserts. Even a section dedicated to my mom, Eileen Potter.

I hope you take the time to go through and see what strikes your fancy! My goal is to have you branch out and try new recipes that are both good and uncomplicated.

Margie Gaunt

Table of Contents

TACO SEASONING – SUGAR FREE

2 Tbls chili powder
1 Tbls smoked paprika
1 tsp salt & pepper
2 tsp cumin
1 tsp each garlic powder,onion powder & oregano
1 tsp Cayenne Pepper

Combine all in bowl and mix. Perfect for any meat or vegetables. Store in container with cover.

I use this a lot on chicken, beef and fish. So good!

ENJOY!

SPICY PRETZELS

1 bag pretzel nuggets
¾ cup vegetable oil
¾ oz dry ranch mix
1 ½ tsp garlic powder
2 tsp cayenne pepper

Preheat oven 250 degrees.

In a gallon size zip bag add pretzels and above ingredients.
Shake well to cover pretzels.
Bake 30 minutes until well toasted stirring after 15 minutes.

Watch out for these! Once you start, it is hard to stop!

ENJOY!

ALMOND FLOUR CHEESE BISCUITS

1 lg egg – room temperature
¼ cup sour cream
1 tsp garlic powder
1/8 tsp Cayenne Pepper
1 cup almond flour
¼ cup grated parmesan
2 tsp baking powder

Preheat oven to 350 degrees. Line baking sheet with parchment paper.

Mix wet ingredients together then add dry ingredients. Mix well. Drop by spoonful onto baking sheet. DO NOT FLATTEN Bake 15-17 minutes until golden brown.

Makes 6 and so very yummy!

ENJOY!

COCONUT FLOUR CHEESE BISCUITS

2 tsp minced garlic
4 eggs – room temperature
1/3 cup coconut flour
¼ tsp baking powder
½ tsp Italian seasoning
4 ½ Tbls butter – melted
1 ½ cup shredded cheese (of choice)
2 Tbls sour cream

Preheat oven 400. Line baking sheet with parchment.

Melt butter and let cool. Whisk together with eggs, salt & sour cream. Add dry ingredients and stir until combined. Stir in cheese. Drop by spoonful onto baking sheet. Bake 15 minutes or until golden brown.

Makes 12

I use these for egg sandwiches. So good!

ENJOY!

SPICY & SWEET MIXED NUTS – SUGAR FREE

¼ cup monk fruit
½ tsp cinnamon
¼ - 1/2 tsp cayenne pepper – to taste
1 cup almonds
1 cup pecans
1 cup cashews
1 cup walnuts
¼ cup Kerrygold Butter – melted
2 Tbls rosemary

Preheat oven to 325 degrees. Line a baking sheet with parchment.

In a small bowl, combine monk fruit, cinnamon and cayenne. In a large bowl, add all of the nuts. Pour melted butter over nuts and stir to combine. Pour monk fruit mixture over nuts and stir until lightly coated. Stir in rosemary. Spread on baking sheet.

Bake 12-15 minutes

So good to put out when you have company.

ENJOY!

CUCUMBER TOMATO SALAD

2 roma tomatoes – diced
½ large cucumber – diced
¼ of a red onion – diced
1 Tbls fresh parsley – chopped
1 tsp red wine vinegar
1 ½ tsp of extra virgin olive oil
Salt & Pepper

Combine all together and enjoy.

*Feel free to add additional spices.

Easy to make and so good for you!

ENJOY!

TOMATO MOZZARELLA BITES

cherry tomatoes – cut in half
fresh basil
mini mozzarella balls
balsamic vinegar glaze
salt & pepper

Using a 4" cocktail pick, thread tomato, mozzarella ball, basil leaf and tomato

Super easy and delicious app to take to parties or while entertaining at home.

*Balsamic glaze is in the salad dressing aisle.

ENJOY!

LOW CARB MOCK POTATO SALAD

1/3 cup sour cream
1/3 cup Hellman's mayonnaise
1 Tbls mustard
2 tsp parsley flakes
½ tsp garlic powder
2 – 12 Oz. bags steamable cauliflower
6 hard boiled eggs
2 Tbls chopped pickles – I use Simply Relish
Salt & pepper

Steam cauliflower per instructions. Spread on paper towels and allow to cool. If pieces are large, cut to desired size. Mix all ingredients in a large bowl until cauliflower is covered.
Add salt & pepper.
Cover at least an hour before serving. I will sometimes make this the night before. The longer it sits, the better the flavor is.

This is so good! I hope you enjoy this as much as we did.

ENJOY!

CHEESY CHEDDAR CAULIFLOWER RICE

4 cups riced cauliflower
1 Tbls Kerrygold butter
½ tsp seasoned salt
3 Tbls cream cheese
2 cups grated cheddar cheese -or desired cheese
Salt & pepper

Optional crumbled bacon

Over medium heat, melt butter. Stir in riced cauliflower. Add seasoning. I use frozen riced cauliflower, so you would want to stir until is becomes hot. About 7-8 minutes. Turn down heat slightly and stir in cream cheese and cheddar. Stir until melted. Sprinkle with optional crumbled bacon. What is better than bacon??

ENJOY!

MUSHROOM & SPINACH RICES CAULIFLOWER

12 oz frozen riced cauliflower
1 Tbls soy sauce
1 Tbls extra virgin olive oil
½ cup chopped onion
minced garlic – to taste
3 cups sliced baby bella mushrooms
2 cups fresh spinach

Heat riced cauliflower according to directions.
Heat olive oil in skillet and add onion. Saute until soft. Add mushrooms and saute until cooked but not mushy. Add garlic and stir. Add riced cauliflower and soy sauce. Stir until combined. Top with spinach and cook until wilted. Just a few minutes.

This is a great side. Super easy and delicious.

ENJOY!

CHICKEN BACON RANCH POPPERS

1 lb Perdue ground chicken – 93/7
½ cup crumbled bacon
½ cup shredded cheddar cheese
1 egg – beaten
1 tsp Herb De Province
1 tsp garlic and onion powder
½ tsp dried parsley
salt & pepper

Ranch dressing to dip.

Preheat oven 375 degrees. Line baking sheet with parchment.

In large bowl mix all ingredients until well combined. I use my hands. Using your hands, roll into equal sized balls and place on baking sheet. Lightly flatten. Bake until golden brown. Usually about 30 minutes.

These are good as lunch or dinner with a side. Or just as they are! So easy to pop in your mouth.

ENJOY!

CAULIFLOWER MUFFINS

2 cups riced cauliflower
½ cup diced onion
1 cup shredded cheese – any you like
1 tsp Herb De Province
Salt & pepper
1 egg – beaten

Preheat oven 350 degrees. Spray muffin pan.

Mix riced cauliflower, diced onion, cheese and spices. Stir in egg. Mix well. Scoop into muffin pan. Press down with the back of a spoon – not flatten. Bake 25 minutes and starting to brown. Cool slightly and gently remove from pan.

Makes about 8-9 regular size muffins.

These gems are so good! You can have them with eggs, lunch or dinner! Get crazy and use different spices.

ENJOY!

CHEESY POTATOES

2 lbs frozen hashbrowns
2 cans cream of chicken soup
2 cups shredded cheddar cheese
1 stick of butter – melted

Preheat oven 350 degrees.

Mix all together in a 13" x 9" pan. Bake
45 minutes until bubbly.

Great side to bring to a family event!

ENJOY!

HEALTHY BEAN DIP

1 can black beans
1 can garbanzo beans
1 can Mexicorn
½ cup extra virgin olive oil
¼ WHITE balsamic vinegar
1 ½ envelopes dry Italian dressing mix
¼ diced red onion
1 pint grape tomatoes
2 avocados – chopped

Mix all together and refrigerate at least 1 hour prior to serving.
Serve with tortilla dippers.

Bring this to a party, and this will become your go to!

ENJOY!

RAMEN NOODLE SALAD

Sauce
¼ cup vegetable oil
¼ cup sesame oil
1 Tbls monk fruit
1 tsp salt
¼ tsp pepper
Sauce Packet from Chicken Ramen Noodles

Whisk together and set aside.

Salad
1 bag coleslaw mix
1 pk Ramen Noodles – crunched up
4 green onions chopped.

Mix together. Pour sauce on, mix well and refrigerate.

Roast 1 bag each of sunflower kernels and sliced almonds.
Cool. Mix in salad before serving.

Delicious and easy!!

ENJOY!

REUBEN DIP

4 cups shredded swiss cheese
18 oz. sauerkraut – drained and squeezed out
¾ cup Hellman's mayonnaise
4 pkg Budig Corned Beef – chopped

Preheat oven 350 degrees.

Combine all ingredients in a bowl. Spread in
13" x 9" pan. Bake 20 minutes. Serve with party rye bread.

This is so good if you like reubens!! I have used this as
dinner and spread it on full size toasted rye bread. Yummy!

ENJOY!

EGG CUPS

fresh spinach
mushrooms - sliced
onion – chopped
chopped tomato – drained*

Layer in the bottom of a sprayed 12 cup muffin tin.

10 eggs
¼ cup milk

Whisk together.

Mix in garlic powder, Herb de Provence, salt & pepper to eggs. Use spices to taste. Pour in muffin tins about ¾ full. Top with shredded cheese of choice.

Preheat oven 350 degrees. Bake until eggs are firm.

This is such a fun recipe to play with different ingredients! Add cooked bacon, sausage or ham. So good and easy!
*I use canned chopped tomatoes w/chiles

ENJOY!

CRUSTLESS VEGETABLE QUICHE

1 Tbls extra virgin olive oil
Minced garlic
1 red pepper – diced small
3 cups broccoli florets – chopped
½ onion – diced small
4 lg eggs
½ cup liquid egg whites
¾ cup milk
salt & pepper
1 Tbls Italian spices
¼- ½ tsp crushed red pepper (optional)
½ cup shredded mozzarella
¼ cup crumbled feta

Preheat oven 350 degrees. Spray a 9" quiche dish and set aside.

Heat fry pan and add oil, garlic, peppers, onion and broccoli. Cook over medium heat until soft. While veggies are cooking, whisk together eggs & egg whites. Mix in milk, s&p, spices. Stir in cheese. Once veggies are cooked pour in dish and top with egg mixture.

Bake 40 minutes or until set. Let rest 10 minutes and serve.

ENJOY!

OVERNIGHT BREAKFAST STRATA

4 slices of bread-torn in pieces
ground turkey sausage – found in freezer section
½ onion – chopped
1 cup milk
3 eggs - beaten
½ cup sour cream
shredded cheddar cheese
Salsa

Spray an 8" x 8" baking pan. Spread torn bread on the bottom.

In fry pan, cook sausage and onion. Drain. spoon over bread. In small bowl, combine milk, eggs and sour cream. Stir in cheese. Pour over meat/bread. Cover & refrigerate overnight.

Remove from refrigerator 30 minutes prior to baking. Preheat oven 325 degrees. Bake uncovered 35-40 minutes or until knife inserted in center comes out clean. Let stand 10 minutes. Serve with salsa.

This really is a great overnight casserole! Love to make it when the kids are in town.

ENJOY!

BISCUITS & GRAVY CASSEROLE

1 lb. breakfast sausage – cooked and drained
1 pk Pioneer Brand Peppered Sausage Gravy
1 cup shredded cheddar cheese
6 eggs
1 cup milk
1 can Pillsbury Grand biscuits
salt & pepper

Preheat oven 350 degrees. Spray 9" x 13" pan.

Cut biscuits into cubes. Line bottom of pan. Scatter browned sausage on top. Sprinkle with cheese. Whisk eggs, milk, s&p – pour over mixture.

Make gravy per package directions & pour over mixture and bake 30-45 minutes.

If you like biscuits & gravy, you will love this!!

ENJOY!

OVERNIGHT FRENCH TOAST CASSEROLE

8 eggs
3 cups milk
1 tsp vanilla
1 loaf Hawaiian Sweet Bread – cut in cubes
Cinnamon sugar
6 pats butter

Preheat oven 350 degrees. Spray 9" x 13" pan. Cover the bottom with cubed bread.

Whisk eggs, milk and vanilla together. Pour over top of bread. Cover and refrigerate overnight.

Before baking, sprinkle top with cinnamon sugar and 6 pats of butter variously placed.

Bake 45 minutes.

If you love French toast, this is such an easy and delicious casserole. Especially if you have overnight guests.

ENJOY!

CHEESEBURGER CUPS

1 lb ground beef – grass fed organic - browned & drained

ADD:
½ cup ketchup
2 Tbls brown sugar
1 Tbls yellow mustard
1 tsp Worchestershire sauce

1 can biscuits
4 oz. Velvetta – cubed

Preheat oven 400 degrees. Spray 12 cup cupcake pan.

Spread biscuits in bottom and sides of each cup to form a cup. Fill with meat mixture and top with cubes of Velvetta.

Bake 12-14 minutes.

This is a family favorite! Quick and easy.

ENJOY!

CHEESY TURKEY BURGER CASSEROLE

1 lb. ground turkey
1 cup milk
2 eggs
½ cup Bisquick
1 cup shredded cheddar
1 onion – diced

Preheat oven 400 degrees. Spray 9" pie pan.

Brown turkey and onion. Whisk eggs and milk together. Add Bisquick mix well. Spread turkey in pie pan, pour egg mixture over top. Top with cheese.

Bake 20-25 minutes.

ENJOY!

SHRIMP CAULIFLOWER FRIED RICE

16 lg cooked shrimp
2 Tbls sesame oil
12 oz. riced cauliflower – frozen
6 oz. peas & carrots – frozen
Minced garlic
½ - 1 tsp ground ginger
3 eggs
Salt & pepper

Heat sesame oil. Add frozen vegetables, garlic & ginger.
Saute about 8 minutes. Add shrimp and warm thoroughly.
Scamble eggs and serve on top.

This is so easy and delicious! Substitute any protein if you do
not like shrimp.

ENJOY!

GROUND BEEF STROGANOFF

1 lb ground beef – grass fed organic
½ onion – diced
smoked paprika
garlic powder
1 tsp oregano
1 tsp thyme
8 oz sliced mushrooms
1 cup beef broth
1 Tbls Worcestershire sauce
½ cup sour cream

Brown ground beef and remove from pan. Add onions & seasoning. Saute about 5 minutes. Add mushrooms and saute until soft. Add broth, Worcestershire & ground beef. Simmer 10-15 minutes. Remove from heat, add sour cream and serve over riced cauliflower.

Yummy, healthy version! So good.

ENJOY!

ITALIAN BEEF W/CABBAGE NOODLES

1 lb 85/10 ground beef – grass fed organic
12 oz. marinara sauce
1 Tbls extra virgin olive oil
Minced garlic
1 tsp Italian seasoning
½ tsp basil
3 cups shredded cabbage

Heat oil in deep fry pan. Add ground beef and brown. When beef is about half browned, add garlic, onion & seasoning. Brown completely and turn to med low.
Cut cabbage in quarters and thinly slice into shreds. Add to meat mixture and stir until incorporated completely. Cover and allow to simmer 7-10 minutes until cabbage is tender. Remove lid and let simmer a few minute to evaporate any liquid.
Top with grated parmesan.

This reminds me of something my grandma would make. Me as a GiGi, make it and they all love! Definite fall dish.

ENJOY!

GREEK LAMB BURGERS

1 lb ground lamb
2 Tbls Worcestershire sauce
1 Tbls extra virgin olive oil
1 tsp salt
1 tsp oregano
½ tsp pepper
1 tsp minced garlic
Crumbled feta cheese

Mix all ingredients together and form 4 burgers.
Grill or fry. Serve with Tzatziki sauce.

If you like Gyros, this will be a treat!

ENJOY!

HEALTHY SPINACH ARTICHOKE CHICKEN CASSEROLE

2 chicken breast – cooked and shredded
2 Tbls extra virgin olive oil
½ cup low fat cottage cheese (NOT fat free)
¾ cup sour cream
2 cups shredded mozzarella
1 tsp kosher salt
1 ½ tsp garlic powder
1 tsp thyme
2 cups fresh spinach
18 oz. artichoke hearts, halved

Preheat oven 375 degrees. Grease a 1 ½ qt. casserole dish.

In a large bowl, add shredded chicken, olive oil, cottage cheese and sour cream. Stir. Add 1 cup of cheese and spices. Stir. Gently fold in spinach and artichokes. Pour mixture in casserole dish and top with remaining cheese.
Bake 40-50 minutes.

My husband was skeptical until he took a bite! Then even had seconds.

ENJOY!

FAJITA CHICKEN CASSEROLE

2 large chicken breasts – cut into strips
2 peppers – one green/one red – cut into strips
1 onion – cut into strips
1 Tbls extra virgin olive oil
1 cup shredded cheese – your favorite

MIX TOGETHER
1 tsp cumin
1 ½ tsp chili powder
1 tsp minced garlic
2 tsp smoked paprika
Salt & pepper

Preheat oven 400 degrees. Lightly spray baking dish.

Place chicken strips in baking dish. Sprinkle half of spices over top and drizzle with oil. Top with peppers and onions, sprinkle rest of seasoning and top with cheese.

Bake 20-25 minutes until chicken is done. Top with salsa & sour cream.

I use frozen tri-pepper & onion blend for quick preparation. This is a winner!!

ENJOY!

CHEESEBURGER CASSEROLE LOW CARB

1 lb. 93/7 organic grass fed ground beef
Salt & pepper
¼ cup chopped onion
½ cup bacon crumbles
Minced garlic
¼ Simply Relish dill relish
3 eggs
½ cup mayonnaise
½ cup half & half
8 oz. shredded cheddar cheese

Preheat oven 350 degrees. Spray 2 ½ qt. casserole dish.

Brown ground beef, onion, garlic, salt & pepper. Drain in a strainer, dump in a bowl. Stir in bacon and relish. Spoon into casserole dish.

Whisk together eggs, mayo and half & half.
Spread cheese on top of meat mixture and pour eggs over top.

Bake 30-35 minutes or until top is brown & set.

This recipe is yummy and low carb!! Winner!

ENJOY!

CHICKEN CAULIFLOWER RICE CASSEROLE – LOW CARB

2 cups shredded rotisserie chicken
12 oz. frozen cauliflower rice
1/3 bacon crumbles
1 tsp Herb de Province or Italian seasoning
½ tsp Kosher salt
½ plain Greek yogurt
¼ cup heavy whipping cream
1 cup shredded cheese – your favorite

Preheat oven 350 degrees. Spray casserole dish.
Mix all ingredients together reserving ½ cup cheese. Spread in casserole dish. Top with remaining cheese.
Bake 20 minutes until hot & bubbly.

Good, easy recipe to make after a day at work!

ENJOY!

Margie Gaunt

STUFFED PEPPERS WITH CAULIFLOWER RICE

3 bell peppers – any color
1 lb ground beef, turkey or sausage
½ cup chopped onion
3 tsp minced garlic
2 cups cauliflower rice
1 ¼ cup chunky marinara sauce – sugar free
1 tsp dried basil
Salt & pepper
½ cup shredded 3 cheese blend

Preheat oven 350 degrees. Spray 9" x 9" pan.

Wash peppers, but in half and remove seeds and ribs. Place in baking dish, cut side up. Sprinkle lightly with salt & pepper.

Brown meat and drain. Pour in bowl – set aside.
Saute onion, garlic and cauliflower rice 4-5 min.
Add marinara sauce, basil, salt & pepper, mix and simmer a few minutes. Stir in meat – heat through. Stir in cheese.
Spoon meat mixture into the peppers. Top with spoon of marinara and sprinkle of cheese.

Cover w/foil. Bake 30-35 minutes.

ENJOY!

PHILLY CHEESESTEAK CASSEROLE

1 ½ lb. 93/7 organic grass fed beef
1 bag sliced peppers/onion blend – frozen
Minced garlic
1 tsp seasoned salt
4 slices provolone cheese
4 lg eggs
¼ cup heavy whipping cream
1 tsp hot sauce
1 tsp Worcestershire sauce

Preheat oven 350 degrees. Spray 9x9 baking dish.

Cook ground beef over medium heat, crumbling as it cooks. When half way cooked, add peppers, onions, garlic and seasoned salt. Cook until beef is done and veggies are softened. Drain and pour into baking dish.
Tear the cheese into small piesces and place over beef. (Feel free to add more cheese) Add eggs, cream, hot sauce and Worcestershire sauce to a mixing bowl and whisk to combine. Pour over beef.
Bake 35 minutes or until eggs are set. Let stand 5 minutes before serving

ENJOY!

AUNT SHIRLEY'S PEANUT BUTTER COOKIES

1 cup Crisco
1 cup sugar
1 cup brown sugar
<u>Cream together</u>
2 eggs
1 tsp vanilla
1 ½ cup peanut butter
<u>Add to above mixture</u>
2 ½ cups flour
2 tsp baking soda
½ tsp salt

Preheat oven 350 degrees.

Mix dry ingredients with the wet. Drop by spoonfuls on ungreased cookie sheet. Crisscross with a fork if wanted. Bake 10 minutes.

These are my families favorite cookies of all!! I want to thank my Aunt Shirley for the recipe.

ENJOY!

IRISH CREAM POKE CAKE

1 box chocolate cake mix – with required ingredients
3 Tbls instant espresso powder
1 14 oz sweetened condensed milk
1 3.4 oz. box instant vanilla pudding
2 cups heavy whipping cream
½ cup + 2 Tbls Irish cream liqueur-I use Kirkland
¼ cup powdered sugar – sifted

Preheat oven 350 degrees. Grease 13 x 9 cake pan.
Combine cake mix & 2 Tbls espresso powder. Prepare
according to box and bake. Cool completely. Use a wooden
spoon and poke holes – 25 (5 rows of 5). Whisk together
condensed milk, pudding, ½ cup hwc and ½ cup liqueur for 2
minutes. Let sit 5 for pudding to set – do not refrigerate. Stir
together 2 Tbls liqueur, 1Tbls espresso until desolved. Whip
1 1/2 cups hwc & powdered sugar with mixer until peaks.
Add espresso liqueur mixture just to incorporate. Spread
pudding mixture over cake making sure holes get filled.
Spread the hwc mixture evenly on top. Chill at least 1 hour
or overnight.

Great for St. Patrick's Day or anytime!

ENJOY!

Margie Gaunt

CHOCOLATE ÉCLAIR CAKE

Graham crackers
3 sm packages of instant vanilla pudding
3 ¾ cup cold milk
1 9 oz cool whip - thawed

Layer graham crackers in the bottom of a 13x9 glass pan. Mix pudding and milk. Fold in cool whip. Spread on top of graham crackers and top with another layer of graham crackers.

ICING
1 stick butter
3 Tbls cocoa
6 Tbls Coca-Cola
1 16 oz. package powdered sugar
1 tsp vanilla

Bring butter, cocoa and Coke to a boil. Remove from heat and add powdered sugar & vanilla.

Pour over top of graham crackers. Refrigerate overnite.

So yummy and easy!! Wow your guests or bring to a party.

ENJOY!

CINNAMON ROLL CAKE

Cake

3 cups flour

1 cup sugar

4 tsp baking powder

¼ tsp salt

1 ½ cup milk

2 eggs

2 tsp vanilla

1 stick butter – melted

Topping

2 sticks butter softened

1 cup brown sugar

2 Tbls flour

1 Tbls cinnamon

Glaze

2 cups powdered sugar

5 Tbls milk

1 tsp vanilla

Preheat oven 350 degrees. Spray 13x9 pan.

Mix all cake ingredients pouring in melted butter LAST! Mix slowly. Pour in pan.

In lg bowl, combine topping ingredients. Spoon evenly over batter. Use knife & swirl through.

Bake 28-32 minutes until done. Whisk together topping. Pour over warm cake.

This is a favorite for breakfast!!

ENJOY!!

CREAM CHEESE POUND CAKE

3 sticks butter softened
1 8 oz. cream cheese – room temperature
3 cups sugar
3 cups flour
6 eggs
1 Tbls vanilla

Preheat oven 350 degrees. Grease & flour bundt pan (do not use spray it will stick).

Cream butter & cream cheese. Gradually add sugar beating well. Add eggs, one at a time. Sift flour. Gradually add to wet mixture beating good. Add vanilla.

Pour into prepared bundt pan. Smooth top. Bake 1 hour or until pick comes out clean. Cool 10-15 minutes on wire rack before removing from pan.
Cool completely.

This is a fabulous pound cake recipe! Delicious topped with berries, cool whip or ice cream!

ENJOY!

ORANGE DREAMSICLE SALAD

1 box orange Jello
1 box instant vanilla pudding
1 cup boiling water
½ cup cold water
9 oz cool whip
14 oz can mandarine oranges – drained
1 cup mini marshmellows

In large bowl, dissolve Jello with boiling water. Add cold water. Chill 15 minutes. Slowly whisk in pudding until smooth. Chill 15 minutes until slightly thickened.
Fold in cool whip, oranges and marshmellows.

Refrigerate 2 hours.

Great, old time salad! Feel free to use any flavor jello and pudding. Mix it up and have fun with it.

ENJOY!

NO BAKE STRAWBERRY CHEESECAKE BARS

<u>Crust</u>
2/3 box of Nabisco Famous Wafers
4 Tbls melted butter

Place cookies in food processor and mix into fine crumbs.
Spray 8x8 pan. Cutout parchment to line bottom of pan.
Spray top of it.
Combine crumbs and melted butter. Press into bottom of
pan. Refrigerate until firm.

<u>Filling</u>
1 ½ cup chopped strawberries
2-8 oz cream cheese – room temperature
¾ cup sugar
½ cup heavy whipping cream.

Puree strawberries in blender. Add cream cheese and sugar.
Blend until smooth.
I separate bowl, beat hwc with mixer until it forms peaks.
Fold strawberry mixture in. Pour into crust. Refrigerate
overnight.

So delicious and light!! Total crowd pleaser.

ENJOY!

PEANUT BUTTER BANANA PROTEIN COOKIES

1 lg ripe banana
1 egg
1/3 cup egg whites
2 Tbls monk fruit
1 scoop Beverly International UMP Chocolate   Protein
1 1/3 cup oats
2 Tbls powdered peanut butter
1/3 cup sugar free chocolate chips

Preheat oven 375 degrees.

Combine dry ingredients in bowl and stir. Add wet ingredients. Mix until combined.

Drop by spoonful on sheet pan. Bake 20 minutes. Cool completely and store in refrigerator.

These are fabulous! Great snack for a pick me up.

ENJOY!

LOW CARB CHOCOLATE CHEESECAKE MUFFINS

2 eggs
4 Tbls cocoa powder
½ tsp vanilla
2-8 oz cream cheese – room temperature
½ cup + 1 tsp monk Fruit

Preheat oven 350 degrees. Line muffin pan with papers.

Beat cream cheese until smooth. Add ½ cup Monk Fruit and all other ingredients. Mix until completely smooth. Distribute in equal parts in the muffin cups. Sprinkle remaining monk fruit on top.

Bake 18-20 minutes. Cool Completely and refrigerate.

Such a guilt-free treat!

ENJOY!

LOW CARB BLUEBERRY COBBLER

3 cups blueberries – fresh or frozen
1 Tbls lemon juice
¼ tsp xanthan gum (or corn starch)
2/3 cup almond flour
1/3 coconut flour
¼ monk fruit
1 egg – beaten
6 Tbls butter – melted

Preheat oven 350 degrees. Grease 9x9 pan

Pour blueberries into pan and sprinkle with xanthan gum and lemon juice. Sprinkle with 1 Tbls monk fruit if desired.

Stir flours, monk fruit and egg until mixture resembles coarse crumbs. Sprinkle over berries. Drizzle melted butter over topping.

Bake 25 minutes or until top is brown.

Yummy!!

ENJOY!

MINI CRUSTLESS PUMPKIN PIE

1 ¾ cup pumpkin puree
2 cup heavy whipping cream
2 eggs
2 tsp cinnamon
½ tsp cloves
½ tsp nutmeg
½ tsp ginger
½ cup monk fruit
¼ tsp salt

Preheat oven 425 degrees. Spray 12 cup muffin tin.

In large bowl, add pumpkin and eggs. Whisk to mix well. Add hwc and mix well. Add spices (+/- depending on your taste), monk fruit and salt and mix well.

Pour in muffin tin in equal amounts. Bake 10 minutes and turn oven down to 350. Bake another 30 minutes. Check with toothpick and when pick comes out clean, they are done. Remove and cool for 15 minutes.

Serve with spoon of cool whip. I could eat year round.

ENJOY!

PEANUT BUTTER CHOCOLATE RICE CRISPY TREATS

4 Tbls butter
4 cups rice crispies
¾ cup peanut butter
12 oz. chocolate chips

Butter 9x13 pan. In large glass bowl, melt chips (in increments of 30 seconds). Add peanut butter. Stir until melted together. Add rice crispies. Mix well. Spread into pan and refrigerate until set.

This is a childhood favorite! I can taste them just looking at the recipe.

ENJOY!

THESE NEXT RECIPES ARE FROM MY MOTHER, EILEEN POTTER.

THEY ARE MY FAVORITE FROM WHEN I WAS A CHILD GROWING UP IN NORTHERN KENTUCKY.

I HOPE YOU ENJOY THESE AS MUCH AS I DID. I HAVE PASSED THEM ON TO MY CHILDREN.

THANKS, MOM, FOR GREAT MEMORIES!!

LOVE YOU!!

CHICKEN & RICE

2 chicken thighs, 2 legs, 2 breast – skin on
1 can cream of mushroom soup
1 can cream of chicken soup
½ can water
1 Tbls minced onion
1 cup uncooked white rice
½ cup diced celery
1 green pepper – diced
1 small jar pimentos – drained
1 can sliced water chestnuts – drained

Preheat oven 350 degrees. Spray 13x9 pan.

Salt & pepper chicken – set aside.
In large bowl, combine ingredients and spread into pan.
Place chicken on top and cover with aluminum foil.

Bake 1 ½ hours.

Brings back so many memories!

ENJOY!

CASHEW CHICKEN

3 skinless/boneless chicken breast – cut into strips
8 oz pea pods (fresh or frozen)
8 oz sliced mushrooms
4 green onions
1-15 oz can bamboo shoots – drained
1 cup chicken broth
1/3 cup soy sauce
2 Tbls corn starch
½ olive oil
4 oz cashews

Cut green onions into small pieces. Put 1 Tbls oil (from ¼ cup) into fry pan and saute cashews. Remove. Add rest of oil and chicken. Cook until done. Add vegetables & chicken broth. Saute until vegetables are al dente'. Top with toasted cashews.

Sooooo good!!

ENJOY!

COMPANY CHICKEN

8 boneless/skinless chicken breast
8 slices swiss cheese
2 cans cream of chicken soup
½ cup milk
16 oz Pepperidge Farm chicken seasoned stuffing
(prepare as directed)

Preheat oven 350 degrees. Spray 13x9 pan.

Whisk together soup and milk until well blended. Spread prepared stuffing on bottom of pan. Place chicken on stuffing and top with swiss cheese. Pour soup mixture over top.

Bake 30 minutes covered then 30 uncovered.

ENJOY!!

CHICKEN & BROCCOLI CASSEROLE

4 lg boneless/skinless chicken breasts - chopped
2-12 oz bags frozen broccoli florets and pieces
1 can cream of chicken soup
1 can cream of celery soup
½ can milk
1 cup Hellman's mayonnaise
1 tsp curry powder
Topping
Shredded cheddar cheese
2 cups Bread crumbs

Preheat oven 350 degrees. Spray 2 qt. casserole dish.

Mix all ingredients together and spread in casserole dish. Top with bread crumbs and cheese on top of crumbs.

Bake 45 minutes.

This is another favorite!!

ENJOY!

RED SPAGHETTI

4 Tbls Margarine (NOT butter)
1 lg onion – chopped
1-6 oz. can tomato paste
1 ½ cups water (or more to make tomato paste a creamy consistency)
1 ½ lb. spaghetti – uncooked

Melt margarine adding onion in sauce pan. Cook until onion is transparent. Add in tomato paste mixture and simmer until spaghetti is cooked. Stir in spaghetti until covered.

This is a great dish for Lent. We had this almost every Friday. To this day, my boys still have my mom make this for them.

ENJOY!

GROUND BEEF, NOODLE & POTATO CASSEROLE

1 lb ground beef
½ chopped onion
1-6 oz can tomato paste
2 cups water
2 lg potatoes diced small
1-16 oz bag of noodles

Brown ground beef and onion in chili pan. Drain. Add in tomato paste and water. Stir well. Add potatoes and cover. Cook until potatoes **ONLY** until they start to soften. Add in noodles (more water if needed) and cook until noodles are done. Top with slices of American cheese.

This was one of my dad's favorites!

ENJOY!

HAMBURGER SPAGHETTI WITH TOMATOES

1 lb ground beef
Small onion – diced
1-15 oz can diced tomatoes
1 small can of sliced mushroom cuts
1 ½ lbs spaghetti – uncooked
Sliced American cheese

In deep fry pan, brown ground beef, onion and mushrooms. Drain. Add in diced tomatoes (with juice) and cook on low. Cook spaghetti. Put back in pot and mix in beef mixture. Top with slices of cheese and put lid on until it melts.

Yes these are all good ole midwestern recipes!

ENJOY!

EASY RAISIN CINNAMON ROLLS

2 cups dry biscuit mix (Jiffy or Bisquick)
½ cup milk
3 Tbls melted Crisco
2 Tbls sugar
Filling
Mix sugar & cinnamon (to your taste)
½ cup raisins (or more if you like)
½ cup melted Crisco for brushing

Preheat oven 425 degrees. Line sheet pan with parchment.

Combine first 4 ingredients to form a soft dough. Roll out into a square. Brush with melted Crisco and sprinkle liberally with cinnamon sugar mixture. Spread raisins on top of dough. Roll up dough like a jelly roll. Cut one inch pieces.

Place on sheet pan and brush each roll with melted Crisco. Bake 10 minutes or until golden brown. Top with icing (Pilsbury vanilla).

Easy, take me back, rolls.

ENJOY!

CPSIA information can be obtained
at www.ICGtesting.com
Printed in the USA
BVHW040205111121
621200BV00016B/960